3rd
generation
AND BEYOND

3rd generation
AND BEYOND

by DANNA PYCHER

ByThisTime
Publishing

By This Time Publishing
www.bttpublishing.com

First Edition

Cover photo:
Sabina & Eliezar Paiczer in Germany two years after WWII ended

Design and Art Direction by Ana Gomez
Cover by Ana Gomez, Israel Pycher and Dan Zacharias

ISBN: 1-480284777
ISBN-13: 978-1-480284777

The words on the following pages are a dedication
to the blessed memory of
Eliezer and *Sabina Paiczer,* my beloved grandparents.
They are the inspiration for many of the life lessons
I have embraced over the course of my lifetime.

In their memory, I would also like to dedicate
this book to the lost souls from both of their families,
who were taken from my grandparents when they were
far too young to be left alone in this world.

In remembrance of the millions of individuals,
victims of the Holocaust, whose fate was sealed before
there was any time to react.

You will not be forgotten.

TABLE OF CONTENTS

3rd generation and beyond

This is for the youth of today – their parents, their future, their dreams.

My hope is that this book will help the younger generations look at life with a perspective that inspires them to create change, speak up for themselves, absorb these important messages and share them with generations to come.

My parents passed down these lessons that I will share with you. They saw firsthand how my grandparents led a life of example.

PROLOGUE

The inspiration for this book came ironically both over the course of 12 hours and instantaneously. The idea first began to formulate while I was in Germany.

Upon graduating college, a couple of friends and I planned to backpack through Europe. I couldn't afford the whole trip, so I told them I would meet them somewhere in the middle. The halfway point we decided on was Munich, Germany.

12 hours...

I landed in Germany rather excited to start my European journey. Upon leaving the airport I was filled with curiosity about what I was about to encounter. The trip consisted of five major European cities. My girlfriends and I would travel by train to each new city. The cities on my itinerary were Munich, Prague, Amsterdam, Paris, and London.

I got to our hostel and my friends were not there. They were elsewhere in the city and wouldn't be back for hours. After getting settled in the hostel and putting my suitcases away for safekeeping, I figured I would take a walk through the town on my own. I seem to have been quite the adventurer! From what I remember Munich was quiet and quaintly beautiful. I walked over to the grounds where the Oktoberfest event was typically held. It was there that I started to get a slightly eerie feeling. I'm not particularly sure if it was the quiet setting that gave me time to reflect and kick start my brain on this non-stop tangent.

I remember I started to feel in my bones that I didn't belong on the grounds where I was standing. It was a very uncomfortable feeling. I turned around, walked away and started back for the hostel. I decided I would just wait there for my friends.

I figured that maybe I felt weird because I was by myself.

I was very happy when they finally arrived. I was starving and thankfully they were hungry as well. My friends Allison and Ashley had plans to connect with some people they met earlier on their trip at the famed Hofbrauhaus.

The Hofbrauhaus is a historical beerhouse in Munich. This pub is also the place where Hitler and his cohorts spent their nights eating and drinking. Hitler ranted some of his first speeches there, which laid out the Nazi party platform that began to plant the seeds of hateful ideology against the Jewish people.

Were we really going to eat there, of all places? I figured it was a historic site, nonetheless.

We met up with Allison's and Ashley's friends whom they had met on the first leg of their trip. Everyone in the beer house was joyous and singing. Then everyone at my table started drinking and celebrating as well.

This is when it all became too much for me. I literally had to leave the pub to catch some fresh air. My friends didn't understand what was wrong. I was overcome with guilt and shame and an overall feeling of nausea. I honestly didn't understand what was coming over me...

Instantaneously...

I was glad to get out of there. We went home to prepare to catch our train to Prague. I was literally in Munich for a total of 12 hours before we left, and I was anxious and relieved to get out.

We almost missed our train. We didn't realize that when people said you need to be on time because the trains leave exactly on schedule, they meant it literally. Germans are known to be very precise and timely.

Thankfully, we made it on board. It was a night trip, so we all went to our cabins to prepare for sleeping.

The train was perfectly comfortable and roomy, but again I felt claustrophobic. I took it upon myself to just look out the window for a while as we passed through the countryside.

When I finally laid down in bed, it hit me. Rather instantaneously.

In the instant that I was lying on a German train I felt as if I was in danger. I didn't intend for any of those feelings to happen, but they did and they were real.

I am years removed from what happened to my family in the Holocaust. I am the Third Generation after the survivors, but am still so affected and even traumatized by their experiences. I never saw or felt even an ounce of what they went through, yet their anguish still coursed through my veins.

Then the idea came to me for this book. My grandparents' stories and lessons created the essence of who I am. It is because I am a Third Generation Holocaust Survivor that I grew to be who I am today. It was their experiences and their lessons that somehow trickled down into my own genetic makeup.

That is when it dawned on me. It is my responsibility to avenge the wrong done to my family's legacy. I am a Third Generation, and with this book I put forth a fight for humankind. I cannot and will not see this happen again.

INTRODUCTION

This is our last line of communication – our eyes. Hers have dulled over, yet they are still comfortably familiar to me.

Sometimes I smile and try to make conversation in a language that is now foreign to her. Sometimes I just sit with her and hold her hand.

There are times I sing to her, in a way that sends shivers down my spine. She actually remembers the tune. We sing together. It's funny, or maybe even a bit tragic. Neither of us remembers the words. At the very least, she has an excuse.

You have to wonder if, in her case, having Alzheimer's disease is somehow a fortunate illness. Alzheimer's erases memory; memories far too harsh and perhaps better off forgotten.

When someone passes, memories remain in the hearts and minds of their survivors. I have plenty of fond memories of my "Safta," as I call her, which is Hebrew for grandmother.

I simply remember her as the kindest woman I've had the pleasure of knowing. Forever giving.

Growing up, I never really understood her. She was always the mysterious grandma who lived far away, one with whom I had to speak to in another language. There wasn't much speaking actually, outside of "Hello" and "I love you." Yet that was enough for her ears.

It became a goal of mine to learn how to communicate with her especially after becoming curious about my family's history. I studied Hebrew in college and that helped a little. But it was still a struggle, not to mention an embarrassment, to try to speak with her. I distanced myself from the discomfort of having a language barrier interfere with the precious bond I felt with her. I decided I could either accept that we couldn't communicate or work on bridging the gap between us.

After college I decided to spend the summer in Israel and learn Hebrew. Finally! I'd be going back to the place of my birth, learning my father's language, and spending the summer in Tel Aviv, which in my opinion is the most magnificent city on Earth.

Alzheimer's disease strikes at peculiar times. Just as I arrived to learn Hebrew, she was forgetting it. I wasn't ready for what I was about to see. She looked old, very old.

The last time I saw her, she still had her life somewhat intact. She immediately offered the entire contents of the refrigerator. She would cook our favorite soup and give us presents, just because.

Sadly, this visit was different. This time she was no longer in the apartment we all grew to love. She was now in a nursing home surrounded by a bunch of other very old people. Cheesy, happy phrases lined the walls to try to fool people into thinking this was actually a happy place.

I approached the nurse who kindly pointed me in the direction of my grandma. I didn't recognize her. Except for the eyes, her magical blue eyes.

They say the eyes are the window to the soul. Her soul must have been exquisite behind those blue eyes. Her entire life is behind those eyes.

There are years of sweet memories. Funny memories. Family memories.

There are memories of war. Abandonment. Bodies lying on the street. Fear. Lies. Hopelessness.

Yes, there are those memories too.

My grandmother is a Holocaust survivor; a survivor of one of the most gruesome periods in the history of mankind. Terror filled the streets as people were selected to be beaten, tortured, or shot to death. Families were ripped apart because of their religion or because of ignorant hatred towards a people who were deemed to have the "wrong" beliefs. Jews, blacks, homosexuals, gypsies, Catholics, political dissidents; no one was safe.

Mass graves throughout Europe hold the souls of millions of desperate people who tried to survive in a time when living was often a worse outcome than death.

Living meant you were left with only the memories of your mother, father, brothers, and sisters who were taken from you. So many people left alone with memories and nothing else.

My grandmother, the only survivor of her family, was left at the age of 16 with only those memories. She survived because she changed her name and was hidden in a farmer's house. Daily life was torture because she was so young and had nowhere to run. She had no one to ask if her mother and father were still alive. Did her brother survive? Why did she survive? For what reason?

When I came to Israel, there were hundreds of questions I wanted to ask her. I wanted to know my history. I wanted to hear about her life before the Holocaust. Where did I come from? Who are these lost souls that are my relatives? I arrived too late...

People asked me how I could communicate with my grandmother. There wasn't much communication actually. Every time, it was her eyes that did the talking. Without words, she spoke. I was moved every time. She spoke for an hour straight just by looking at me.

It's because of those blue eyes that I wish to pass on her life lessons. I wish for her wisdom to reach to the ends of the world and back. But, if her wisdom touches just one person, my mission is complete.

Safta, this is for you....

life lessons

KINDNESS

"The highest form of wisdom is kindness." -THE TALMUD

The ultimate lesson to learn is that kindness is everything. Everything.

The simple notion of being kind to someone can completely alter the way a person proceeds with the rest of his or her life. Smiling and being nice to someone can save a life. It saved mine and in return, I have unknowingly saved others.

When I was 12 years old I had a friend, Rachel, who told me that simply because I was friendly to her, I gave her the confidence to talk to other people. I was astonished when she told me this. In middle school I didn't know how to put myself together, let alone put a brush through my hair. Yet, this girl admired me. She told me she was intimidated by me because I seemed to make friends easily. She wanted to see if she could be one of my friends. Being welcoming by nature, I took her in. That single moment changed her life, forever.

Sometimes when I'm having a bad day, the simple act of a stranger smiling at me can immediately uplift me. It's a weird phenomenon. I may not even know this person, but I know that smiles are contagious. This stranger's smile started a chain reaction that I brought into the grocery store. The people around me carried that smile into their own apartments. Their friends in turn smiled when they set out for the night. That one unassuming smile was felt by many people. Such a simple, effortless gesture can change the mood of the day and the world around you.

My grandmother would tell our family a beautiful story about a chance encounter with a hunchback person during the war. She was in hiding on a farm with a Christian family in Poland. One day on her way to bring milk to the local market, this hunchback midget on the street abruptly stopped her. He told her to turn around immediately because the Nazis were killing Jews down the street. She took his advice and abruptly went the other way. How he sensed that she was Jewish we'll never know, but that small act of bold kindness literally saved her life.

When you are open to other people's kindness you realize there is really so much to learn. Give a little bit of yourself and you will get a lot in return. I promise. Pay a compliment where it is due. Tell a friend how much you love them. Be daring and help an elderly stranger walk up the steps.

Kindness is infectious. Spread the disease.

APPRECIATE
WHAT YOU HAVE...NOW!

"Make it a habit to tell people thank you.
To express your appreciation,
sincerely and without the expectation
of anything in return. Truly appreciate
those around you, and you'll soon
find many others around you.
Truly appreciate life, and you'll find
that you have more of it." – RALPH MARSTON

We are all too familiar with this mentality: In twenty years I will have the big house with the white picket fence, the husband/wife, the kids, the dogs, the cars, and so on, and so on, and so on...

Here is where this line of thinking is "off." There are so many things we have in our lives now that we need to be thankful for. Number one on the list is family, that is if you are fortunate enough to have a family. There are plenty of people out there who don't. There are those who come from abusive families, broken families, families filled with hardships and tragedy.

The people I have met in my lifetime who come from less fortunate situations are usually immensely more grateful for what they DO have, as opposed to people who appear to have it all.

It's all about an appreciation of your life; for your health; for your mom, and for your dad. If you don't have any of those at the moment, take pride in yourself because you made it in this world on your own.

My grandfather came from a large family that included seven brothers and sisters. Although his father had a successful business, he had a family of nine people he had to feed. It was necessary for their family to be resourceful.

My grandfather was one of the youngest children. His older siblings were mostly girls.

A famous tale he used to tell my father was that he had to wear his sisters' hand-me-down dresses until he was 8 years old. He didn't have a choice because this was what his parents could provide.

He used to tell that story with pleasure because it was a lesson he learned at a young age: to appreciate that at least he had clothing on his back.

Life can be tough. It's a struggle EVERY DAY for some people. What makes it worth pushing forward is recognition and gratitude for the little things.

Thank everyone for everything. If someone drives me somewhere, I say thank you. If there is food on the table that my mom merely stuck in the microwave for 30 seconds, I say thank you. If someone hurts me and I learn from the experience, I ultimately say thank you.

Your life is your perspective. Be thankful for what you have. Be thankful for what you don't have. At the end of the day, it's the hardships in life that make us truly appreciate the good. The harder it is now, the sweeter it is tomorrow.

Appreciate the sweet and sour flavors of your life.

FEAR IS AN ILLUSION

*"Always do what you
are afraid to do."* -RALPH WALDO EMERSON

All animals, including humans, have the hormone adrenaline. It flows through the body when we need an extra kick of energy. When a lion is chasing a zebra, the zebra will exert a lot of adrenaline in order to save its life. This is called the "Fight or Flight Syndrome." Fear is a tool the body uses to produce adrenaline in case of emergency. Fear is an emotion used for protection and can be very useful in times of danger. Otherwise, fear should be put away because it can be inhibiting to all aspects of our lives.

The exciting part about life is that you can experience something new every day. Most people don't take risks because of fear of failure. Most people don't approach that attractive person because of fear of rejection. Most people don't get to know people of a different race because of fear of the unknown.

Forget fear. Only in the case of an emergency, remember it. In every other circumstance, give risk a try.

Some of the best experiences I have had in my life come from putting myself out there. My biggest fear is stage fright. I'm a singer and it takes a great deal of persuasion for me to perform for someone. Though when I finally do perform, my biggest fear becomes my greatest joy. There is nothing more exhilarating than having a risk pay off. Life can get pretty monotonous otherwise.

One of the most profound stories my grandfather told was of the day where everything in his life changed. It was the day of selection in the Warsaw ghetto where his family was living for that part of the war. Selection in the ghetto meant one thing. It meant deportation to the death camps. On this terrible day, it was his family's turn for selection.

His family was gathered at the Umshlagplatz, the train station where Jews were rounded up for deportation on trains to their final minutes of existence on Earth. In the moments leading up to boarding the train, my great grandfather, Israel Meir, looked at his sons and told them to run.

"Run away as far as you can go," he told them.

He said, "I have to stay here with my wife and small

children, but you two are young and have to run."
Against every feeling they had in their minds, they ran away.
In that heartbreaking moment, they ran for their lives.

That was the last time my grandfather and his brother
Leon saw their family. They were shot at and chased after,
but they fled and made it into the forest.

In that instant, my grandfather made his most life changing
decision. He left everything and everyone he knew behind
in the small chance he could make it out of hell alive.

His risk is the reason I am here today. I am forever
grateful. Yet, I often think about the split second decision
and wonder what I would have done. It's a thought I wrestle
with a lot.

Byproducts of fear are racism, hate, jealousy, and even
murder. All of these are sparked by a fear or ignorance.
Why do so many people hate others that they have
never even met? It almost always comes back to ignorance.
What a shame.

People use fear to manipulate each other.
Fear is a figment of your imagination.
Be fearless.
Take risks.
I dare you.

DON'T LABEL ME

"I think fitting in is highly overrated.
I'd rather just fit out... Fitting out means
being who you are, even when people insist that
you have to change. Fitting out means
taking up space, not apologizing for yourself,
and not agreeing with those who seek to label
you with stereotypes." –GOLDA PORETSKY

"You're Jewish? You don't look Jewish. You certainly don't act Jewish."

I never really understood what people meant by all of that. I think they were complimenting me in some twisted way. Well, here's the thing. I AM Jewish. I am white, tall, thin. I have curly hair, although sometimes I wear it straightened. I'm half-Canadian, half Middle Eastern. Sometimes I'm wearing makeup, often I'm in gym clothes. I can dress like a hippie or like a professional. Every day, I decide who I want to be. Other people don't. So, do me a favor, don't put me in a box. I am ME. I am unique and no matter what label you find next, you still won't get me.

People like to assign labels. It's more comfortable for some reason to place people into certain categories. Get to know someone by looking beyond their label and the pre-conceived notion or stereotype.

Businesses make millions of dollars by selling you their brand or their label. People at the top of their industries are making massive amounts of money off of us because we are slaves to labels. Let's not put people in the same categories.

During the Holocaust, the Nazis put the Jewish people under one label. That label of "Jew" meant one thing: Death. The Nazis literally had to contrive a definition of what a Jew was in order to enact their mission of getting rid of the Jewish people as a whole.

The fact that my ancestors were "labeled" Jewish sent nearly all of them to their deaths. The fact that my grandmother was labeled a Catholic during the war, saved her life. The fact that my grandfather's brother Leon looked like a "Christian" saved him numerous times during the war. His Aryan look often gave him the privilege of blending in and being able to see yet another day. My grandfather didn't have that luxury and was often afraid to be out of hiding because his "Jewish look" would give him away in a heart beat.

During the war if you were lucky enough to get false papers, you could change your identity. Therefore, your new false label could potentially save your life. Labeling can do some seriously strange things.

Don't let someone else define you. You are you, and that's just fine.

LIVE THE WAY
YOU WANT TO...NOW!

"Your time is limited, so don't waste
*   it living someone else's life. Don't be*
trapped by dogma - which is living
*   with the results of other people's thinking.*
Don't let the noise of other's opinions
*   drown out your own inner voice.*
And most important, have the courage to
*   follow your heart and intuition. They somehow*
already know what you truly want to become.
*   Everything else is secondary."* – STEVE JOBS

Why is living life the way you want to so intimidating?

What's so scary about doing things your way? Are we taught to be just like everyone else? I think we are.

The people who make the biggest difference in the world are the ones who do things differently. Their way is the only way, and in the process they are shaking everything up.

You were born to a specific set of parents, in a specific environment, in a specific body; all unique to you. How are you supposed to live your life like everyone else, when you cannot possibly be anyone else but yourself? There is a reason you were born as you were. You have to fulfill your destiny, and a good time to start is now.

There are a million reasons to not live the way you want. Society makes conforming to be like everyone else seem like it's the right thing to do. If that is the way you see your life, then there is nothing wrong with that. It's perfectly okay. If it's not the way you see your life, then it's not okay.

Circumstance plays a large role in how your life unfolds. If you are born into a poor community, then there are many resources that may not be available to you. Sometimes the richest people succeed because they are born poor and they learn the value of working hard to get what they want. Every circumstance you are in, whether it is positive or negative, is an opportunity to grow.

As a little girl, I always wanted to be a performer. Many people recognized my talent, but I was never fully supported in thinking that singing was a "practical" way to make a living. Society tells us that creative work will never pay the bills. It was hard for me to battle all these voices saying that I couldn't do it. For years I battled between my "practical" life and my creative life. Then the day came when I almost lost my life in a near fatal car accident that left me handicapped and bedridden for a long time. From that day on, I forgot the word "practical." No one else's voice mattered to me anymore. The only voice that mattered was my own.

I went back to school to study music and fulfilled one of my lifelong dreams of singing in a café. Not only was the music so imperative to my dreams, it was actually one of the most "practical" components in my healing from the accident.

Many believe that there is little or no choice in the way your life pans out. In reality, you know what is best for you in your life. You can feel it. Life is too precious to waste your time listening to other people's voices.

Do yourself and everyone around you a favor. Live your life, your way.

THE ACCIDENT:
MY DARKEST HOURS

It was a clear, blue day in sunny Florida. I was on my way to meet my friend for ice cream to catch up on what was happening in each other's lives. We had been distant for a while and we wanted to change that.

I was ready to head out when my friend called and asked that I wait a little while longer because she was running late. Typical! She is our "notoriously late" friend. We changed our meeting time from 2:00 to 4:00 PM.

On my journey to finally meet her, I was driving through a shopping plaza when I realized the center where I actually needed to be was across the street. I drove up to the stop sign at the edge of the plaza and fully stopped to see which plaza was the correct one. Just at the time when I saw the ice cream store across the street where we were supposed to meet, a car came charging at me at 80 miles per hour.

I had no idea what happened. One moment I'm stopped at a stop sign, the next my car is flipping onto a main road.

The car flipped three times before it finally landed upside down. As I was flipping, all I kept saying to myself was, "Oh, my G-d, I didn't do anything. I didn't do anything."

I wasn't driving. I wasn't texting. I was just minding my own business, sitting at a stop sign.

When I finally realized what had happened to me, this overwhelming feeling of pain washed over me from the middle of my body down to my legs. The first thing I did was wiggle my toes to see if I was paralyzed. My toes moved and this gave me confidence. I couldn't go anywhere because I was stuck upside down, trapped underneath my steering wheel. All I could think to do was to yell out my mother's phone number.

Soon there were people outside of my front window looking in at me. It must have been horrifying for them to see me crushed inside my car. I just kept on shouting my mom's phone number.

Then a man jumped onto my car's passenger side and stuck his hand through the window to support my neck. That is when I finally heard the reassuring sound of sirens. Help was on the way.

My car was smashed around me and the firefighters were at a loss as to which way was best to get me out. At this moment no one knew if I was paralyzed, so it was of utmost importance not to cause any further injuries.

The firefighters spent at least 30 minutes arguing about

how to release me while I was hanging upside down trapped inside my mangled car. For the majority of the time I was relatively calm. Then as the time ticked by I began to lose my cool. I started crying to the firefighters that I would do whatever it took to be removed from under my steering wheel, if they could just cut me out the back of my car.

That is exactly what happened. I used all of my strength to move my broken body from underneath the steering wheel. The first image I saw when I was finally out of my car and on a stretcher was my mother. She was red in the face, hysterically crying as she was running up to see what happened to me. I mustered what strength I had left to give her a "thumbs up," letting her know I was going to be okay. The last thing I wanted was for her to be a patient in the hospital bed next to me.

From that moment, my life was literally turned upside down. In an instant, I was hit. That instant turned into thirty minutes, which later turned into years of rehabilitation, both physically and mentally.

I broke my pelvis in multiple places leaving me physically handicapped and bound to a wheelchair until my broken bones could mend. Thankfully, we found out I wasn't paralyzed. I had broken the bone directly underneath my spine. If the break had occurred just half an inch higher, I would certainly have been paralyzed.

For the first few months after the accident I was in a

wheelchair and then later used a walker. I never imagined that I would be in a wheelchair so early in the game of life.

Interestingly, people treated me differently when I was in the wheelchair. They smiled at me for no reason. They actually made eye contact with me instead of avoiding eye contact with a stranger. Strangers wanted to help me. What a nice change!

On the flip side, never had I felt more dependent on people in a negative way. I couldn't go to the bathroom unless my mother assisted me by taking off my clothing. As a 24- year-old, having to be undressed by someone else was a very painful and humbling experience. I no longer had the free will to do as I wanted; to do as I needed.

A successful day consisted of me being able to shower and brush my teeth on my own. I had to relearn every skill I had once taken for granted.

I also hit my head in the accident. As a result, I became a lot slower mentally. I had to work every day on my cognitive skills. My biggest concern after the accident was that I would lose my greatest gift, my ability to think.

That is just a glimpse into my long, long road to recovery.

In my darkest hours, the theme that kept playing through my head was that I was a descendant of Holocaust survivors and that it would be unfair of me to give up my fight to survive. There were times I contemplated ending my life, and again I was reminded that my grandparents survived in order for me to live. It was unjust of me to take everything away from them that they fought so hard to preserve. I am the descendant of people who would not quit, no matter what. Who am I to give up so easily?

My grandparents survived harsh winters without food, shelter, or loved ones that they could count on for comfort. Every day their survival was solely dependent on their own will to see another day. Their dark hours, I'm sure of it, were darker than anything I could encounter in my lifetime. Their perseverance was what I looked up to in my time of doubt. They are the ultimate role models in my life.

I learned so much about life, perspective, and the bigger picture over the course of those two years after the accident. I could fill another whole book with the lessons I took away from just that time. But for now, let's start with this one...

JEALOUSY. ENVY. ANGER.

*"Anger is an acid that can do more
harm to the vessel in which it is
stored than to anything on
which it is poured."* -MARK TWAIN

It might seem odd, but I had never experienced the emotions of jealousy, envy, or anger until I was in my mid-twenties. I had a conversation with a friend who once said in disbelief that that was impossible. She asked if I was ever in a situation in which I was jealous of a friend for something they had achieved. I answered easily, "No, I haven't. The only person I've ever been jealous of is Oprah Winfrey. I want her job."

When I was younger, the emotions I tended to experience were sadness or confusion. If someone wronged me, I would get upset and look at him/her and wonder to myself why or how a person could be like that. It wasn't natural for me to get angry. I literally never had the heat of anger as part of my being.

It isn't as if I chose to be that way, I just dealt with disappointment in an internal way. I never blamed others for what they did. I always looked for a way to understand where they were coming from.

All of that changed the months following my accident. Anger was suddenly all I knew. I was angry with the man who hit me and caused me such suffering. I was angry with my friends for not understanding my pain. I was angry that I was stuck in a wheelchair and there was nothing for me to do but wait for the day that I would not have to be angry anymore.

Feeling anger was so hard for me. It was such a violent feeling. I wasn't used to feeling such internal heat. I didn't want other people around me to succeed. I no longer wished the best for everyone. I wanted people to be in my shoes. I wanted them to feel what I was feeling. How unfair is it that I was broken inside and out and everyone else could go on with their lives.

Where was the justice? It took me a long time to shift to these new feelings. I did a lot of internal searching in order to understand why I no longer wanted other people to be happy.

I look back now and think how selfish I was. I wasn't going anywhere in my life and I wanted that for other people. How shameful.

Experiencing jealousy, envy, and anger made me realize how harmful these emotions were, not only to me, but to everyone around me.

I still harbor these emotions sometimes, but I try to keep myself in check. It's natural when you feel stuck in life to look at others and envy their successes. What has to be clear is that your day will come.

Life is like a wave that ebbs and flows. For all the drawbacks there are fortunes. For all of the dark there is light. It's taking the tough situations in stride that makes you a survivor.

My grandparent's perseverance was the ultimate inspiration for me to move past all of my negative feelings. In order to keep on living a normal, fulfilling life, they had to move forward with their thoughts and feelings and learn to be happy with what life they had at the moment. I often thought about them and used their life example for inspiration. My grandmother was perhaps my deepest inspiration. Every time I saw her, she appeared to me like a ball of light. Even after everything she went through, she still maintained her positive glow.

READ TO GROW

"To read is to fly: it is to soar to a point of vantage which gives a view over wide terrains of history, human variety, ideas, shared experience and the fruits of many inquiries." –A. C. GRAYLING

Life is about learning and growing. It's constant. This is one thing you can count on and it's a good thing! We learn through everyday experiences, our education, and our own pursuits of knowledge.

One of the best ways to learn is through reading. The ability to read is a gift one should not take for granted. Reading is the portal to a better life. Guaranteed.

Through reading it is possible to see the world. Not only can you see the world from your bedroom, you can envision what it looked like in Medieval Times when kings and queens decided the fate of the land. Through reading it is possible to discover alternate realities and live through the eyes of others. Not only are you able to free your imagination by reading, you can obtain other people's perspectives and use them for your own success. You can literally learn to be anyone or do anything.

Throughout history, books were burned because people in power deemed the books controversial. These people knew that when someone read a book, they were given the power of knowledge and free will. In the United States, during the period of slavery, black people were denied literacy because if they were able to read the newspapers and abolitionist writings they would feel more free to revolt against their slave masters. Reading was a powerful tool that sometimes gave way to a slave's freedom.

During the Holocaust, Jewish texts were burned as a way of degrading the Jewish people. One of the most infamous nights of the Holocaust and one of the first major acts of mass violence against Jews, was called Kristallnacht, also known as the Night of Broken Glass. On this night, many Jewish homes and synagogues were raided and burned, with only the "shards of the broken glass remaining on the street." People were dragged into the streets and beaten until they either died or remained a living pulp. The Nazis also made a spectacle of burning Jewish books on this night. It was supposed to symbolize the eradication of Jewish culture and religious freedom of thought. The burning of books was a major blow to the Jewish people and their culture because the foundation of Judaism is the Torah, the Jewish bible, and its surrounding literature. In fact, the Jews are known as "The People of the Book."

Again, reading is not only symbolic of freedom; it is a means to freedom.

Reading enhances creativity and strengthens the mind. If I didn't read, or have the passion for knowledge obtained through reading, this book would never have been written.

KNOW YOUR HISTORY

"A people without the knowledge of their past history, origin and culture is like a tree without roots." -MARCUS GARVEY

Although they claim she didn't know me, somewhere deep down I am certain that she did. Seeing her in this weakened state in a nursing home where she was surrounded by dying elderly people didn't make it any easier. Despite all that, I cherish these moments. I see myself in her.

I would take my grandmother outside to sit on a hill to overlook the view. We sat on a balcony overlooking the city of Haifa, with the crystal blue sea in the distance. I tried to give her half an hour of tranquility every visit. We would just sit there and look out. This was the least I could give her.

I would hear her saying little phrases like "shaine maidele," meaning pretty girl, and "git," meaning good, which gave me hope that she enjoyed these moments as much as I did.

Every time I would leave her side I would get this sense of strength, as if she was trying to channel her power over to me. We somehow had this unspoken connection.

I liked to visit her because I tried to learn as much as I could about where I came from; who I am. She somehow gave me a better sense of where I was going as well.

One of the most gratifying experiences I've ever had was the chance to visit Poland, and explore my ancestor's hometowns. In those few days, I learned so much about myself.

It was a turning point in my life. I saw the quaint farm towns my grandparents grew up in and I discovered many stories about what happened to my family. One particularly astonishing story that really connected me with my ancestors happened on this trip.

My parents and I, along with our Polish tour guide Alec, visited the town where my grandfather came from. It's a small town outside of Warsaw called Mszczonow.

We were trying to track down my grandfather's history, but were at a loss as to where to start. It occurred to my mom to ask the old men sitting on a park bench if they knew anything about our family. Bear in mind, these were random men in their eighties, drinking beer in the early morning in the middle of a park. We approached them nonetheless.

Our tour guide asked them the simple, yet powerful question: "Do you know the Pycher family?"

One man jumped up and exclaimed, "Do I know the Pycher family? Who doesn't know the Pycher family?!"

We were in shock.

He continued, "The Pycher family used to own the horse and wagon company. I used to work for them. When I was a young boy of 13, I fed their horses hay! Let me take you to their house."

Now we were in utter shock.

We followed him a couple of blocks down to an old house with an old stable. He told us that this was the one house that wasn't burned down by the Nazis during the war. My family and I looked around and all of a sudden I see the address on the house. The house was number 18. The number 18 is both my birth date and my lucky number. It was then that I broke down in tears. I was intrinsically tied to this house and my history.

I believe that when you learn where you come from, it becomes clear who you are and who are you are meant to be.

BE A SURVIVOR.
GET BACK UP.

"Nothing could be worse than the fear that
one had given up too soon,
and left one unexpended effort that
might have saved the world." -JANE ADDAMS

The key to success is failing. This may sound counterintuitive, but it's true. The great achievers in this world have all gone through trials and tribulations in order to get where they are. People who learn to accept failure as part of the process of life are more able to succeed in the end.

Failure is the BEST tool to learn why you didn't succeed this time around.

The world is created in a way to give you the right tools to set you up to win. The more trying experiences you have, the more knowledge you have to do it better the next time.

If you don't fail, it means you haven't risked. The only way to truly know if you lived your life to the fullest is to take risks. These risks are called calculated risks. These are risks where you have something to gain, such as knowledge, friendship, or experience.

So many people are afraid to take risks because of the possibility of stumbling along the way. They are afraid of rejection or even the possibility of humiliation. In reality, everything ends up working out the way it is supposed to. It all eventually falls into place. What's meant to be will be.

You are meant to take risks, because your life is meant to be extraordinary.

With every experience you have in your life, try to take a life lesson away from it.

There were many periods in my life where nothing seemed to be working out for me. I would take three steps forward and then fall five steps backwards. My life was falling apart and I didn't understand what to do. Why was this happening to me?

I had a conversation with a family friend, Liora, who looked at me straight in the eye and said, "Say thank you for everything that happens to you and everyone who brings you down. Say thank you, because in the end these people and these hard times are what shape you and make you who you are." That life lesson has stuck with me ever since.

Learn to survive the periods in your life that are tough.

Know that every life lesson that tries your strength and brings you down is preparation for the next big step in your life. Trust that the hard times are meant to test you. They are only tests, not permanent situations.

Learn to survive with grace and gratitude; the grace to get back up and the gratitude to say thank you for every life lesson.

DON'T BE
TOO SCARED TO HELP!

*"That best portion of a good man's life;
his little, nameless, unremembered
acts of kindness and love."* -WILLIAM WORDSWORTH

Whenever you are in doubt about helping someone, please help. Don't rely on others to take action. Step in. Do something.

People are mistaken in thinking that they aren't responsible for helping others in need. Some think it's none of their business and they have their own problems to deal with. Don't buy into this. Even the smallest gesture can help.

I was attending my high school's homecoming dance, having the time of my life, when I happened to encounter a girl falling over ill in the bathroom. Everyone in the bathroom was staring at her or was too busy to care.

I could not believe my eyes. Not one person moved to help. I immediately ran to tell someone to call 911. I knew I couldn't help her with my own hands, but at least I could start the action. Who knows if she would have made it, if it weren't for that small action I took to get help to the scene?

If it weren't for the people who stepped out of their cars on the fateful day of my accident, I may not have made it. I think of these few special people very often. I still don't know their names and I never will. This does not matter. They helped save a life. From that day forward, these nameless people are my heroes.

I'm never afraid to help someone. Even if it means standing up for someone or something that is unpopular. Now, I always speak out. What does it matter to me if someone thinks I'm weird or too opinionated? Over time when you speak out to help someone or support a cause, even an unpopular one, people will come to recognize that you are right.

Sometimes negative consequences can come from helping. In every situation, it is important to stand up for what is right.

My father told me magnificent stories of my grandfather's inclination to help others. Often, when my grandfather would walk down the street, random people would come up to him to say thank you. He would get stopped all the time, almost daily. My father didn't know exactly why so many people stopped my grandfather, yet he knew that he was very charitable with his words of advice and even his money. He was so generous to others. He always found it difficult to say no to someone in need.

This generosity didn't stop with people only in his community. My grandfather did business with people across all cultures. It didn't matter if the person was Jewish, Christian, or Muslim; my grandfather was always willing to help.

My parents told me that when my grandfather passed away there were hundreds of people at his funeral. Again, people from all walks of life no matter what their belief, appearance, or religion, came together on the day of his funeral to commemorate a man so respected and admired.

My grandfather knew that if you put out positive action in the world, one day, positive effects will come back around to you.

Don't just stand there, reach out and help someone.

FRIENDS FIRST,
BUSINESS SECOND

*"Don't walk in front of me, I may not follow;
don't walk behind me, I may not lead;
walk beside me, and be my friend."* -ALBERT CAMUS

In this day and age, we are taught to be selfish. It's survival of the fittest, really. In capitalistic societies the only way to survive is to be greedy and claim what is yours. We lose sight of a very important concept on the way to capitalistic success. You don't get anywhere on your own.

It's rather unfortunate how we have become socialized to put ourselves first. It is important to remember those who are good to you and are supportive of your endeavors.

They say it is never good to mix business and friendship, because ultimately the friendship will suffer. The same has been said for involving friends with finances; money ruins friendships.

I have found that one of the most important relationships in life are those with close friends; those handful of people whom you can rely on unconditionally.

If a friend is truly sincere and caring, they will want what's best for you in your life and career. If you are careful in selecting a friend to partner with in a business opportunity or endeavor, that friend should enhance the relationship rather than destroy it. The true test often comes to light when disagreements appear. As in any relationship, it is how a disagreement is resolved that matters.

After the war, my grandparents had no surviving family. Their friends quickly became family. My grandfather was quick to bring his friends into his business whenever he could. His business was a means to an end. He needed to make money in order to survive. Beyond that, if his friends could be involved and make money too, there was no sense in being competitive. His ultimate happiness came from sharing whatever he could.

BE KIND
TO YOUR NEIGHBOR

*"To love our neighbor as ourselves is such
a truth for regulating human society, that
by that alone one might determine all the
cases in social morality."* –JOHN LOCKE

It's the oldest rule in the book. It is preached in many religions. We even call it the Golden Rule. "Treat your neighbor the way you want to be treated."

My father grew up with a lady named Scheindel, whom he called Aunt. In reality though, she wasn't his aunt. She wasn't even related to him. Scheindel was a big part of my father's life growing up. She was like a second mother. She was infamous in my father's household for her cooking and her ability to make butter and yogurt from scratch.

Scheindel lost everyone she knew in the war. She left Poland and came to Israel to start a new life. She searched for people she knew who might also have immigrated from her home-town of Amshinov, Poland, to Haifa, Israel. She came across a handful of people, but no one came to see her. When my grandfather heard that she was looking for people, he immediately went to see her.

Scheindel was my grandfather's neighbor. She lived down the street from him in his childhood hometown. He saw she had nowhere to go, so he told her to come live with his family. She was hesitant, but later having nowhere to turn, accepted his invitation.

This woman became one of the most influential people in my father's life. Although she wasn't technically family, she was the closest thing my father ever had to experiencing an aunt.

The building blocks of a good community all start from the smallest gesture of respect for the people who are living right next to you. Because your neighbor is so close to you, learning to share your space is necessary.

All actions start small and eventually grow to what they are meant to be. Learn to cherish yourself and your neighbors.

CONNECTEDNESS

"The important element is the way in which all things are connected. Every thought and action sends shivers of energy into the world around us, which affects all creation. Perceiving the world as a web of connectedness helps us to overcome the feelings of separation that hold us back and cloud our vision. This connection with all life increases our sense of responsibility for every move, every attitude, allowing us to see clearly that each soul does indeed make a difference to the whole." –EMMA RESTALL ORR

We are all connected in one way or another. It's hard to grasp or feel at times, but it's true.

What you do today not only affects you and the people around you in the present, but it also affects the lives of those to come in the future. If you subscribe to this belief, it gives you, as an individual, such power to bring good into the world. It is everone's responsibility to realize this connectedness early on so it becomes a global mission to help bring light into this sometimes dark world.

My grandfather didn't know how his life would turn out. He didn't know if he would make it out of the war alive. His perseverance and strength during and after the war shed light on those around him. He survived the majority of the war by hiding in the forest. His survival allowed good to overcome evil in this world and for that reason, I believe good does overcome.

It's like skipping a stone on a lake. At first the stone makes a big splash and you expect that afterwards it should sink. Yet, it doesn't. It creates a beautiful ripple down the line, time and time again. Although smaller and not as present, the first action made an impact on the second, third, and fourth splash.

You see connectedness in nature in the way animals interact. You see it in music in the way one song, like a national anthem, can connect a nation. You see it in humankind in laughter and tears.

You are as connected to me, as I am to you. When this simple idea is realized, its impact could be universal. Everything I do can have an effect on you. Everything you do can and does affect me.

QUESTION AUTHORITY

"It is the first responsibility of every citizen to question authority." –BEN FRANKLIN

It's nice to believe that those in authority know best. If only that were the case.

Just because someone is a figurehead or is somehow in a position of authority, doesn't mean that they are going to be just or do the right thing. Oftentimes, when a person comes into authority, he or she will start to abuse their privileges.

It is every person's utmost responsibility to question authority. Questioning authority doesn't mean disrespecting your elders or questioning everyone who is in a position of power, but rather knowing that even the people in charge must be held accountable.

Never again should we let a people be persecuted by the hands of a governing body. We said "never again" after the atrocities of the Holocaust, yet we still see murder at the hands of oppressing governments, even in our times.

Many musicians and artists challenge authority through their work. It is not uncommon to see political commentary in the form of lyrics in a song. Even though it may not seem like a big action, in truth when people hear the music, the messages are also heard loud and clear.

Everyone now knows the Earth is in orbit around the sun. This is an undisputed fact. Yet, when Nicolaus Copernicus, a Polish astronomer in the time of the Renaissance period, first came up with this theory, he was challenging all of the world's prior thought that the sun actually revolved around the Earth. This outlandish theory that he came up with infuriated the Catholic Church because of its contradiction to existing religious dogma. The church denied that this new theory had any truth or merit. Yet, Copernicus stood firm with his "insane" theory despite all of the odds. Where would the rest of the progression of science be if it weren't for this one man's conviction that even though no one else believed him, his theory that the Earth revolved around the sun was accurate?

History is full of examples like that. Until someone has enough audacity to challenge the current system, nothing will change. Of course, it isn't always necessary to change what is already in existence, but if a change needs to be made even one person that has the courage to do so can change the status quo.

Don't be afraid to be a leader and take charge if you feel that those in charge aren't being responsible. Some of the most powerful revolutions started with only a small group of motivated individuals. It is a shame to ever feel like you are too small to do something.

LITTLE THINGS

*"I still get wildly enthusiastic about little
things... I play with leaves. I skip down the street
and run against the wind."* -LEO BUSCAGLIA

My grandfather used to love to talk about this cherry bush
he had when he was a kid growing up in Poland. Whenever
the cherry bush was mentioned he would light up.

What's so exciting about a cherry bush? To my grandfather, this bush represented so much more than little,
red, plump fruit. This cherry bush was a representation of
his childhood and family. To some people a cherry bush
is nothing more than a shrub that produces fruit, but to
others this same shrub can mean so much more.

Sometimes in life the love of little things gets so
obscured by the need to collect bigger and bigger objects. We
have become a society of collecting the latest and greatest,

when in reality the little things like playing a game or going outside for a walk with friends and family have become less cherished.

When I was little, one of my favorite times spent with my grandmother was when she would polish my nails red. When I say red, I mean fire engine red, nothing a typical child would wear. I loved every second of it.

Just sitting there with her while she held my hand and painted each little finger is a memory I still hold dear. It's important to take a step back and really take hold of the little things that make this life so precious.

Little red cherries, little red nails...big memories.

PERSPECTIVE

"You cannot control what happens to you,
but you can control your attitude toward
what happens to you, and in that, you will
be mastering change rather than
allowing it to master you." -SRI RAM

Life is all about perspective. One person who is blind, living in isolation on an island, can ironically view life as more beautiful than someone who seems to have it all, vision included.

Perspective is of the utmost importance. You have a choice. You can go through life believing that your life is in the pits and you have it bad, when someone else could look at you and envy the life you live. Or you could view your life from a greater, positive perspective. Sometimes all that needs to change is your viewpoint.

A great way to gain perspective is to read about other people's cultures, and if you are fortunate enough, travel anywhere around the world. Experiencing different cultures and settings can give you beautiful perspective into what life really is all about.

My Safta, oddly enough, with all she had been through, always had a beautiful perspective. Even towards the end of her days when she was asked how she was feeling she always said she was doing well. Although her health was failing, she was alone in her nursing home, and her memory was slowly leaving her, she always said she was doing okay. And in her perspective, for some reason, all truly was well. I very much admire that.

Today should be the day where you change your life compass to face north and have a forward thinking perspective. Next time you have a bad view, actively work on the angle in which you are looking at your life.

DON'T WAIT TO VISIT
PEOPLE WHEN THEY ARE DEAD

*"I just wish I could have told him
in the living years"* -MIKE & THE MECHANICS

I would give anything to have had the chance to know my grandfather, however he died a few months after I was born. I've heard so many legendary stories about him that I feel as if I know him, although we never did meet.

People tend to take others for granted until they no longer grace this earth. It's so important to recognize those who are important to you while they are still here.

So many people congregate at funerals to say lovely things about the now departed. If only those lovely things were said to the person while they were still alive!

Don't visit people when they are dead. Make an effort to see friends and family while they can still smile at you from across the room. Even if you are estranged, no one is ever too far away from a phone. Try to make things better.

After I was in the accident, my friend relayed a story that changed her life. When I didn't show up to meet her as planned, she started to get nervous. She heard there was a rollover accident up the street and when it occurred to her that it could have been me, she began to worry. She called the police and they confirmed her worst fears. They wouldn't tell her if I was dead or alive, just that I was on the way to the hospital.

For an hour she thought I was dead. She feared that not only did she not get the chance to say goodbye, she felt devastated that I left this world when she and I were not on good terms. There would be no second chances.

She told me that what happened that fateful day not only changed my life, it changed her forever. She thought she would only get to say her apologies at my funeral.

Thankfully, it didn't end that way.

My beautiful grandmother, Sabina Paiczer.
She continued to smile throughout her life despite
all of her loss.

My grandparents loved to dance.

My grandfather's biggest joy was laughing with his family.
Here he was putting his hat on my brother's head.

My great grandfather's house in Poland. It was the one house on the street that somehow wasn't burned down by the Nazis. The Polish residents of the town told us this story.

My grandfather used to speak about the little cherries that grew in his backyard that he loved as a kid. He never went back to Poland after the war and never saw his childhood house again. On our trip to trace our family's history in Poland we saw the cherry bush he used to speak about.

18 is my lucky number. It also happened to be the address of my great grandfather's house in Poland.

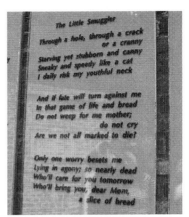

My father and our tour guide, Alec, showing us Ghetto Warsaw. The ghetto held over 400,000 Jewish people in only a little more than a square mile area of land. My whole family was in the ghetto. My grandfather smuggled my grandmother out of the ghetto after the Nazis murdered her whole family. She was only 16 years old at the time.

The famous poem "The Little Smuggler" written by Henryka Lazowertowna. You can see my dad's and my reflection on the glass.

My father and I signing the guestbook outside of the Treblinka Death Camp. The majority of my family was murdered here in the gas chambers. My father wrote name after name of lost family members. Unfortunately, I didn't recognize a single name.

Safta and I. My inspiration.

PATIENCE, PERSISTENCE, PERSEVERANCE

"Life is not easy for any of us. But what of that?
We must have perseverance and above
all confidence in ourselves. We must believe that
we are gifted for something and that
this thing must be attained." -MARIE CURIE

I often wonder what was going on in my grandmother's mind while she was in hiding.

She was a teenager, about 16 years old, when her family was torn from her. Her whole family was murdered. She was a young girl, all alone.

My grandfather, although they were not married at the time, was told by his parents to sneak her out of the Warsaw ghetto. He did as they said and left her in a Polish farmer's house promising the family gold and money if they hid her until the war was over.

I can only imagine what must have been swirling through her mind as the one person she knew in the world left her with strangers. I'll never know, but I know she lived with patience, persistence, and perseverance.

She lived every day, waking up in the morning with no knowledge of what was to come for her. A few years went by with my grandmother acting as a Christian maid in this family's house.

In everyone's life there is a point of questioning. Why am I here? What will be tomorrow? What is the purpose of all of this? I can imagine her asking the same questions. Although she had nothing left to live for she had the hope to survive for a better tomorrow.

With patience, persistence, and perseverance anyone in the world, no matter what the circumstances, can achieve his or her dreams.

Even if these dreams are only of survival.

MEMOIRS

"I've given my memoirs far more thought than any of my marriages. You can't divorce a book." -GLORIA SWANSON

Write your memoirs. Remember your dreams for they are all that can build tomorrow and all that can recall an image of the past.

I wish I had memoirs of my family. Little things. Things like how was it everyday living in their small town. What were the conversations like? Who told the jokes? Who cried every Shabbat at the beauty of lighting the candles? Who was the backbone of the family? How was it to be alive so many, yet so few generations ago?

I never kept a diary. The few snippets I have of my life are often recorded only in dark times. I'm sure they would make for good reading to family down the line.

Writing is a beautiful way to connect with those no longer here. I long to write. I long to read.

By writing memoirs you can revisit times in your life when things were tough, challenging, fun or frustrating. You can speak of love and pain or rejoice in simple pleasures that made you smile.

I recommend you share your inner thoughts. Someday they will mean so much to someone. Even if it's only you.

I know that in my personal memoir I will include some of the poetry I've written over the years. Poetry, for me, has always been an outlet of expression and emotion especially when I don't know the exact words for how I'm feeling. I write poetry for personal growth and satisfaction and rarely do I share it! I would like the future generations of my family to have a peek into my inner thoughts, though.

This is a poem I wrote one day while I was thinking of my Safta. Thoughts of her and my ancestors often evoke a poetic response.

JULY 20, 2008

Pretty blue eyes; don't recognize
the tears from my smile.
If only you knew what I would give
to go back awhile.
To the time, where red splashed your lips.
The memory rips,
from the back pages, of my script,
which will never be complete.
Because your pretty, blue eyes,
don't recognize

Here is another poem I wrote about Israel, which is also known as the Land of Milk and Honey. I believe that my ancestors had dreams of Israel and would have given a lot to go to this distant land. I am writing from the perspective of a dream.

There is a land out east
where the black clouds part
and the mountains descend from above.
Where the water smells like orchids
and the sky bleeds morning light.

This land out east
calls to me
hymns of a foreign tongue.
Chanting to me.

There are treasures yet to discover.
I'm yet to awaken to what I'll find.
One day I'll return to the Land of Honey
and internally I'll find my treasure.

Until then

This land out east
calls to me
hymns of a foreign tongue.
Chanting to me

GRATITUDE

*"At times our own light goes out and is rekindled
by a spark from another person.
Each of us has cause to think with deep
gratitude of those who have lighted
the flame within us."*-ALBERT SCHWEITZER

My father used to say something very peculiar to my brother and I when we were growing up. He used to say, "If your mother puts rocks on the table for dinner, you will eat them and say thank you."

As an eight-year-old, I thought my father was a bit weird for saying that. I later learned what that funny saying meant. It's the same quote that my grandfather used to tell my father. What it means is that if there is food on the table, even if your mother isn't the best cook, you should be grateful. Well, my mother isn't the best cook, but over time what I learned is that I need to appreciate the fact that I was fed.

Gratitude is a gift. I remember when I was younger, I wasn't very aware of how to be thankful for what I had. Being grateful was something I learned. I was taught the concept of gratitude over time through my grandparents' odd, yet very wise expressions.

As I've grown older, I've realized how important having gratitude is. There are hundreds of ways to look at life situations. I actively choose to look at all of my ups and downs with a grateful outlook. It makes the ups sweeter and the downs more bearable. I always say to myself, what will I learn from the down this time? I also think about how great the up is going to feel when I overcome the obstacle. It's not easy to think this way, but it ultimately makes for a happier life.

IF ONE WAY DOESN'T
WORK, FIND ANOTHER WAY

*"Most success springs from an obstacle or failure.
I became a cartoonist largely
because I failed in my goal of becoming a
successful executive."* -SCOTT ADAMS

In almost every audition of my life and career, I was nearly always the runner up. I was never noticed first. In middle school, I was the first alternate cheerleader. In high school, I was the runner up for the TV news anchor position. Yet, in both scenarios, through my hard work and effort, the teachers in charge noticed that I was talented and eventually chose me over the other talent.

Now in my professional life, knowing that I'm notoriously terrible at auditioning, I try to supersede this process. Instead of attending auditions I aggressively contact producers and essentially tell them to hire me. These producers keep me in mind if they have projects coming up in the future. What I have done is find an alternate way of getting hired. I did this with my strengths and weaknesses in mind. Anything is possible. It's all about maneuvering and finding different ways to achieve your goals.

A legendary story about my grandfather happened when he lived in Israel after the war. My grandparents moved to Israel in 1951. In that time Israel was facing a major economic depression. My grandfather couldn't speak the language, he was in completely new surroundings, and he couldn't find permanent work.

A year after my grandparents moved to Israel, my father was born. At this time my grandfather still had a lot of problems making money. He had no car so he had to get a cab in order to bring his wife and his son home. He ended up getting a loan from a friend just so he could pay the taxi driver. He promised that he would pay back the loan when his business took off. He took my father's birth as a good omen for a new life in a new land and he knew internally that he would find a way to pay this loan back.

His business did end up taking off and my grandfather was good on his word. He started raising cows and selling them. He now had money and would look to pay back everyone that helped him along the way.

If one angle doesn't work for you, that doesn't mean your goals won't come to fruition. If a door is closed, climb through the window.

Create your opportunities. Create your reality.

LONG LIVE YOUR LEGACY

*"I'm not looking for a legacy, and you'll never
shut up the critics. I've been around
for 50 years. When you're a catalyst for change,
you make enemies - and I'm proud of
the ones I've got."* -RUPERT MURDOCH

People live magnificent lives, and all of a sudden their lives
and their legacies are gone.

What better gift can there be than to leave behind a legacy?
Whether it be in the form of a short penned expression
of kindness and wisdom to family and friends, or a long
thought provoking book, or a cause near to your heart; let
your life live on. At the end, all that is left is a legacy. This
doesn't need to be intimidating in nature. Just something.
Everyone should have the chance to live on after passing on.

I wish for my legacy to be wise words and inspiration for

people in need. I wish for my legacy to bring to this world a bit more goodness and kindness. I wish to be remembered as someone who cared and gave a damn.

Our time on this earth is so very brief, and no one knows when that time comes to an abrupt end. Each and everyday we are given a clean slate to start anew. We are given the opportunity to paint a canvas of our lives with an endless palette of choices. The legacy we live and the one we leave behind is a combination of each day of our existence; a landscape of life.

Since the accident, I feel more empowered to live each day to the fullest. I cannot help but think what may have happened had I met my friend a few minutes earlier or later that day. Fate was that I was in the wrong place at the wrong time, but I lived to tell my story. And hopefully I lived to inspire others to view life as an opportunity to find the goodness through the pain. That is what my beloved grandmother did just by living in a kind, gracious, and inspiring way.

FILL THE WORLD
WITH MUSIC AND DANCE

"Hitler is gone. The Nazis are no more.
Yet, we are still here.
Singing and dancing." -SIMON WIESENTHAL

There is nothing that invokes more emotion and passion as an art form than music.

Fill the air with music. Hum and sing whenever you can. Play music in your home.

My grandfather used to love to dance. It was one of his little life enjoyments. He would fill the room with his playful dancing and spirit.

Everyone that knew my grandfather fell in love with him. He had such a joyous personality that made everyone want to celebrate life. He would invite the whole neighborhood over for Shabbat dinner. If he met someone new that week, he always made sure to invite him to his house for a special meal.

His spirit was always dancing, and when he danced in front of others their spirits danced too.

My parents said it seemed as if one thousand people came to his funeral when he died. His little acts of welcoming and kindness made the whole town want to get to know him, and when his time came, the whole town came to his gravesite to pay respects.

I can sometimes imagine the music he danced to. It would be something of a waltz from the 1920's. It would be just him and my grandmother in a room with the music surrounding them and nothing else. I imagine that these were his moments of sheer happiness.

HATRED
IS HEREDITARY

"Hatred is something peculiar.
You will always find it strongest and most
violent where there is the lowest
degree of culture." -JOHANN WOLFGANG VON GOETHE

It's a rather simple concept. Children aren't typically born with innate hatred; it's a learned behavior. It can be passed down socially from generation to generation. As a Jew, I have witnessed many acts of anti-Semitism out of the mouths of young people. Even if they said in a quiet undertone that they were "just kidding," I know in reality that there is an element of truth in their words. Where did they learn to hate Jews at such a young age if not for their ignorant parents who told of our "horns" and other damaging stereotypes?

When I was a child, the worst case scenario with "hateful"

kids came about on the playground or in a catty fight between jealous girls. Now hatred rears its ugly head in ways that kill. I'm always shocked when I read about yet another case of a school shooting or random rampage of violence involving innocent bystanders. Then there are the countless stories of bullying that cause irreversible harm, sometimes even death by murder or suicide. It always makes me ask the same question. Where did these people learn to hate and how did we let our hatred go this far?

It's easy to pass down hate and ignorance. The challenge is to teach members of society to teach compassion.

On that note, when a person starts speaking in a hateful way, tell him/her to shut their mouths. Say it harshly. Don't let anyone continue speaking when what they are saying is hateful.

The words that come out of your mouth have the power to create reality. So if someone is spewing out hateful words, don't hesitate to think they will act in a hateful way.

The Holocaust is the epitome of what hatred can do. The Jewish people as a whole were submitted to cruel and unusual treatment by the hands of people who hated them for the sole reason that they were taught to hate them. They were tortured, experimented on, and killed for what reason? Why did six million people have to die and countless others have to go through daily torment?

It all starts and ends with unchecked hatred.

RESISTANCE

"I agree with Dante, that the
hottest places in hell are reserved for those who,
in a period of moral crisis,
maintain their neutrality." –MARTIN LUTHER KING JR.

There was resistance to hatred in every circumstance during the war- physical, mental, and spiritual resistance. One of my hot buttons when people speak of the Holocaust is their tendency to believe that the Jewish people just laid down and submitted to the Nazis' hatred. This couldn't be farther from the truth. These people lived every day making decisions in which somehow they were resisting the terror that surrounded them.

Stories from Holocaust survivors inspire the generations that came after them. Yet, we forget that the people who tragically perished were fighters as well. Even in the smallest instance of reciting the Shema, the most central prayer in Judaism, in the darkest of hours was a form of resistance. This resistance says, no matter what you think you can do to me, you cannot strip me of my identity.

It is my plea, that if you take one thing away from this book, it is that you must resist evil. Every act of resistance, no matter how small, can change the course of history.

You must not be silent.

EPILOGUE | MY WISH

It is my wish that this little book you are holding in your hands be the catalyst for change in our societies. It is a big wish, I know, but it is ultimately my highest wish. If we can't foresee a better tomorrow, then what is the point of today?

It is my wish to see individuality flourish even under the draws of conformity.

It is my wish to encourage open debate and discourse. Agreeing to disagree as long as both sides are open to growth.

It is my wish to see the youth of today ask questions, speak out, and find the commonalities between us rather than the differences.

I may be the Third Generation, but you are the Fourth, the Fifth, and the Sixth. All of us are survivors.

Question. Resist. Be Kind. Those are my wishes...

ADDENDUM

While I was exploring my roots in Poland a few years back, I wrote a handful of emails to my friends so they could keep up with my journey. This trip was the first time I realized that I liked to write. Without the confines of having to be grammatically correct because they were just casual emails to friends, I was able to write freely without feeling hindered by writing "correctly." Here is a sampling of the emails I wrote describing my family trip in Poland. Please, forgive the grammar! I am keeping the emails in their original form. I wrote them when I was 21 years old.

Poland...Mixed Thoughts
August 5, 2007

Hello Friends!

Only on my first day and already I am over-whelmed with thoughts. Getting to Poland was an adventure in itself. Chaos.

It took me about 1:45 to get to the airport. My driver took the long way to JFK. You know, for fun. I get a phone call from my mom saying, "You won't believe this, our flight is canceled." By that time I was 12 mins away from the airport. I get there and my mom is waiting on this lengthy line and my dad is waiting by the luggage. It's great to see them.

My mom told me to go up to the side of the line to find out what is going on and of course they were speaking Polish so I was lost. I then saw a woman go to the front of the line and proceed to speak in thicker Polish. What happened then was everyone that understood her got out of line to give her their passport. I was confused by this. What I later found out was that she said she had 15 spots on another flight and she offered this to the first 15 people that gave her their passports. GREAT! The whole line got messed up and that's when the disaster started.

I went up to the lady to find out what was going on. I asked her to speak in English. She wouldn't. The two Polish women behind me started to speak to me in a tone that I gathered was disgruntled. I told them I didn't speak Polish and they said I skipped them in line, how could I. Then one of the woman's husbands started to speak to me, and tell me how disrespectful I was. I had no idea what was going on. He kept talking to me in a condescending way so that's when I picked up my serious 'who do you think you are talking to' tone. He wasn't expecting that. I told him I didn't speak

Polish and he proceeded to say, "Well I speak Polish and English." I told him he was great. He told me I needed to get behind him and the rest of the line. So, being obnoxious, I told him and the rest of the line to get in front of me. I was understanding, but he was rude in the sense that I was clueless and he just kept on talking.

So the managers of the airline had no clue how to handle the mess. Everyone was yelling about who cut who and I haven't felt surrounded by so many dumb people in such a long time. ANYWAY! We ended up booking a flight for the same night on Air France. We had great food on the airplane, including brie cheese. I really liked this airline.

I ended up taking a Dramamine to help me sleep. Of course it didn't kick in until an hour before the plane is landing. I was up squirming all night uncomfortably. Every seat had an individual TV that had games on them as well as the normal TV/film programming. I learned how to count in

French and my mom and I played Mah Jong. So, this whole time I'm cursing the dramamine until it finally kicks in and then I seriously cursed the dramamine. I feel like jelly still. I was sooo knocked out I started sleeping on everything I could rest up on. I had to take a nap. But everyone knows I love those.

I woke up and my parents and I went walking around the city. The hotel we are in is central in Warsaw and really nice. My mom keeps on asking me if I want to check out the gym. I'm baffled as to why she was asking me and why she wanted to go herself. As if she really cares. ANYWAY... We walked around this cute little shopping area. H&M, Zara, Espirit was here. All the American advertising and even the Simpsons movie is out here already. I felt very at home in my modern surroundings. When you continue to walk through it starts to look more like it should. Old brick buildings that towards the bottom are covered in cement to help solidify the foundation. My dad kept talking about the different architecture, telling me what's old and new.

We were on a mission to find this one recommended restaurant (which we didn't even eat at) in the old town. All throughout there are little ice cream/gelato/coffee shops. It started to feel more old town European the more we walked into the city. Cobblestone all over the place. I told my dad we had to get some ice cream because the soft serve didn't look normal. (more on that later) We ended up eating at this place with "authentic polish" cuisine. We had cold borscht soup (amazing), pierogies filled with sauerkraut and mushrooms (also amazing) hot dogs on buttered rolls and potato gnoche-like balls. Not everyone would love what we ate, but I, of course ate it all and was entertained by the new tastes.

I felt awake for the first time during dinner when I drank my dad's beer. This was fun of course b/c my mom kept telling me I shouldn't drink it b/c it'll make me sleepy. We sat next to these patrons that just sat down to drink vodka shots, midday. My dad and I then got the ice cream I was so curious to try. I could taste the butter fat. I loved every authentic second of it. Real food, real fat, really great!

We passed by a few monuments. One of Copernicus, which I wanted a pic of but none of us had a camera at the time. We passed by another monument called the Fallen Soldier. There were all these Israeli & Polish soldiers standing at attention. My dad asked what was going on, and they said once a year the two armies honor the Resistance against the Nazis. It was really cool to see.

We then started back to our hotel. That brings me here to my email. Which I sadly am addicted to. My mom is once again begging me to go see the gym with her. I'm going to go do that. It'll make her happy for reasons unclear.

Thank g-d for wireless internet!

Tomorrow I'm going to see the Warsaw Ghetto. This is when my true experience will start.

My dad told me that my grandpa said that Pollacks do not question what they are told and in that sense they are dangerous people. I viewed some of that today while in the airport. It was eery. I felt lost in communication and bewildered at the idiocy of the people I was surrounded by. (to be blunt) I will see tomorrow, up close and personal, of how the extent of doing exactly what you are told can cause the destruction of so many.

Those are my thoughts! :)

Travels...Lengthy you are warned!
August 6, 2007

Friends,

We handled it well. We had to meet our tour guide at 9 am. So, in order to be prompt, we woke up at 6! We decided to eat at the breakfast buffet. The meals here consist mostly of smoked fish and other interesting items. The buffet was international though, including crepe-like pancakes.

After breakfast, Alec Moldysz, our tour guide came to our hotel, to meet us. He is a very elderly, yet knowledgeable man. My dad and him got along quite well. He immediately began to spill all of his thoughts. We told him where we wanted to go and what we wanted out of the trip.

Today, we made a few stops. Most of what is left are monuments of buildings demised or statues representing notorious people. The first stop was the only remaining wall of the ghetto. The ghetto all together was about 2 miles. It seemed pretty big, because we had to drive from landmark to landmark, but when you think about it, many thousands of people were locked in this area. The last remaining wall is standing solo, but is attached on one short side to new residences. The only reason this little portion remains is because a survivor, a non-Jew, who lives nearby after the war, refused to let anyone touch it.

Poland is a living memorial to World War 2 and it was evident with every sight we saw. Most of the remnants are incorporated into modern residences. After visiting the wall, we went to old tenements. These apartments back in the day were nice properties, and now the people that live in them pay very cheap rent. It is mostly young people that live there. Alec told us that most of the residents don't bother to renovate for fear that one day the true owners will come back and kick them off the property. I wonder if people do come back to these little apartments to claim them. Is it worth it?

One of the buildings we saw was once a textile factory and now it is still being used for manufacturing, but not sure of what. My dad said it was possible that my grandma worked there. But, we don't know anything for sure. It was once again a reminder that modern day Poland is still embodied with old remnants of a brutal history.

So, I am trying to film a lot of my trip for possible editing later. I want to maybe create a little newsy documentary about my time here. We'll see. If anything it'll make for recorded memories. I asked my mom to shoot a standup for me. I am learning to hate standups and I think the more I do it, the cheesier they feel. So I did what I thought was an ok standup.

Alec earlier in the day showed us a picture of the little ghetto, where people worked, being connected to the big ghetto, where people lived. We took notice of the picture and then continued on our way. He then, unknowingly to us, took us to the exact site. (This is where I did my standup, because I thought it was captivating. lol) All you could see now was one of the buildings on the little ghetto side. The bridge and the big ghetto weren't there anymore.We looked from picture to sight and it was really intense. Pictures are living history, and even that history can change.

Our next stop was an 100 acre cemetery. You had to pay admission to help upkeep of the grounds. So many ornate tombstones. The cemetery is from 1805 and a lot of the tombs had intricate sculptures or stories of ones life or livelihood. My mom was taken by a specific one that reminded her of a tree stump with a flowery vine up it. Alec told us that a cut down tree symbolizes death. We then began to see more tombs like it. I never thought that tombs could be so showy. In an eery sense it was like an ancient art gallery. Alec showed us some prominent people throughout the cemetery. Actors, writers, politicians, martyrs, many more. Towards the end of the cemetery journey we came across a children's Holocaust memorial.

This is the first place I teared up. There was a brilliant poem written by a child in the ghetto. I don't remember all of it, but in the end the boy tells his mom not to cry or worry about him, because he worries about her and getting her some bread. There were some famous pictures of Holocaust children, including Anne Frank.

Alec then took us to 'Mila 18'. This was the place of the last stronghold of the ghetto uprising.

A few hundred young people within the ghetto wanted to die with dignity, so with the few pistols and knives they had, they tried to fight back. The memorial was a rather large stone on top of a hill. The other memorial to these people was more impressive. It was a little up the road and was in two parts.

One was a sculpture representing the young people as strong fighters, when in reality they were famished and struggling. The other which hit me hard, was a replica of a sewer. The last surviving of the uprising made it out by traveling the sewers.

Umshlagplatz is the center of some of my Dad's stories. It is the train station that took Jews to the death camps. It is here where my grandfather saw his dad for the last time. My grandfather was told to take his brother and run, and not to look back. For this reason, he escaped the train, only to never see his family again. This, like all the others, is now only a monument. The walls had all the Jewish first names of the people that went through. So many stories...

My father was quiet for the first time, while sitting in a place that is so inherent in who he is today. I could go into detail for so many sights and thoughts... That is for a later date... To sum up, the other sights we went to were an infamous orphanage which housed a famous teacher, Janusz Korczak, who was allowed to go free, but went to the camps with his kids, and the only surviving synagogue. (which was beautiful and currently being renovated)

If you got all the way through this..I give you props! My thoughts are with you :)

Enjoy your afternoon!
dp

The poem I saw that day is one of the most famous poems from the Holocaust. I feel as if I should share it, because it embodies the pain of the time from the eyes of a child. The poet's name was Henryka Lazerowtowna. She and her mother she writes about were both killed in the Treblinka death camp.

The Little Smuggler

Through a hole, through a crack or a cranny
Sneaky and speedy like a cat
I daily risk my youthful neck

And if fate will turn against me
in that game of life and bread
Do not weep Mother - do not cry
Are we all not marked to die?

Only one worry besets me
Lying in agony; so nearly dead
Who'll care for you tomorrow,
Who'll bring you, Dear Mom, a slice of bread

HENRYKA LAZEROWTOWNA (1909-1942)

Everybody knows Paiczer!
August 7, 2007

Gien Dobry (Greetings!),

Growing up, I'd always ask my dad to quiz my brother and me in trivia. We would sit at the dinner table and my dad would fire off history questions. I loved this for multiple reasons. For one, my dad instilled a passion for history in me while I was young. Secondly, it was one game I had a chance in beating my brother in! My father's thirst for history, I think, inadvertently sprung from his lack of knowledge about his own history. This would change today...

We visited two small towns, once even smaller villages, outside of Warszawa. The first town is where my grandfather spent his youth. A quaint town named Mszczonow (pronounced Moshinof in polish and Amshinov in yiddish).

As we drove in, our first stop was going to be City Hall. My parents had a different opinion though. We saw three elderly (two drunk, one medicated) men sitting on a park bench. My mom told my dad that it might be a good idea to ask them if they knew of the Pycher (Paiczer) family. One of the men sprung up and exclaimed, "Pycher? Everybody knows Pycher!" He proceeded to tell Alec (our guide) and my father stories about my family before the war. He told us my family owned a horse and buggy company, which at the time was the only transportation from town to town. This was a lucrative business that employed many of the people in the town, including Urek, the man we were speaking too. Urek used to bring hay to the horses. He then suggested, to our surprise, that he could show us the very house.

The beginning of this day was very emotionally moving. I was slightly shaky, (ok, I'll be honest my camera work is not the most stable in general) due to being choked up.

Urek, on his bicycle, showed us the way to what was my ancestor's house. Every house in this town seemed fairly new. (More on this later)

We approached the house and it was the only one on the street that looked as if it was from the 1900's. The property was large and included what was once probably a stable.

This was OUR house? As I mentioned yesterday it is possible to reclaim your land. But this house seemed more of a living memory then something I'd want to renovate, or live in, or sell. But it was ours. Alec told us of a lawyer who could help us reclaim our land. It was one of the largest properties in town. But the house itself was rundown and dirty. As I also mentioned yesterday, people do not renovate for fear of the rightful owner coming back. Will we reclaim? I doubt it.

Just seeing the property slowly made scattered

stories come together. We met a lady that lived in a little house on our property. She was very nice to us and helped us with our questions. Her address was 18a. Our address was 18. If you know my fascination with the number 18 you will understand the impact this had on me.

After much discussion and overlooking the area, we left to go buy Urek and his buddies some beer. We went to a little corner store and bought a few beers. (and an ice cream :))

On our way back to the old men we came across a few more elders. What they had to say was interesting as well. The old women said that after the Jews were sent to the ghetto this little town was burnt to the ground. Only one street survived. Only a few houses. Only one on the right side. That house, was my great-grandfathers. Ironic, that 60 some odd years later, my family would come full circle to see our house. It still remained, although worn from years of disregard, it still stood.

We then went to the place where all the documents were stored, since City Hall is being "renovated" to look the way it did before the war.

We found a small excerpt stating my grand-fathers birth. We took pictures for documentation. On our way out of town we went by the house again. We took a piece of wood off the house and a stone from the surrounding area.

Then we traveled a little ways to my grand-mother's town Wiskitki. (Viskit in yiddish) At first we thought we wouldn't find anything. We went to this town's City Hall and were abruptly told that they were sorry and that there was no documentation.

Alec later told us that the Jewish papers were put in a separate place upstairs. The women said if she had time tomorrow she'll look upstairs.

We then tried our luck again and asked the oldies in the town. The first was a muttering drunk, the second was new to town, the third was a man with a hat that was a little more informative. He told us of an 80 year old women that knows everybody in town. Oddly enough, my mom took a picture of this colorful house earlier on the drive and it ended up being her house.

She wasn't home, but we ventured into a little room nearby her house (very sneaky) and we uncovered that she was some kind of clairvoyant. We're on the right track!

We were advised by her neighbors that she was probably in the field and we should come by later. We then went to find the Jewish cemetery to see if my dad could recognize some last names. This site was impossible to find. We tried the Russian graveyard a few times until we asked some locals that finally knew.

The cemetery was all grown over with tall grass and weeds. It seems as if no one cared about the people buried here. There were a few cracked tomb stones. One my mother and I saw lying flat on the ground and we peeled the dirt off of it.

We then tried again to find the old woman. We went back to her house and fortunately we found her son-in-law. He offered to take us to her in the larger town of Zyardov. She was very confused at first, but then offered to take us back to Wiskitki to show us some landmarks. Minute by minute she seemed to piece together who she thought my grandmother was.

She took us to a corner sklep (or store) and told us that that is where the old synagogue was. Most of the Jews in town lived around the square surrounding the synagogue. She then lead us to a red door and said, "There."

We still aren't sure if that is where she lived, but my father said he felt strongly as if it was...

Once again, details have been left out. I'm not sure if you can imagine what today felt like. I hope you can see why this trip is so important to my family. Slowly we are learning who we are...

Treblinka

This is probably my last email from Poland, considering the last stop of our custom tour was yesterday. It took a little bit for me to find the words for yesterday, so here it is!

The Polish countryside is truly beautiful. There were storks throughout the area. The Poles say that they bring good luck. We had to drive a couple hours (a little less than two) to get to the camp site. All along the journey our guide, now George, was telling us some facts about the war in general. I took advantage of this time to sleep, with one ear open.

He said a few interesting points, but whenever there was something that piqued my curiosity I would ask questions. One thing he mentioned of interest, was that there were a significant amount of concentration camps in France during the war, but it was not considered PC to mention those after the war due to France's involvement with the Allies. He said France was more than just cooperative with the Germans, they were instigators. I did not know that! He also mentioned that only three countries in ALL of Europe did not have an SS unit. One of those was Poland and the other two I forget. They were small countries though. Every country was involved, even if it was minimally. It's funny how history tends to clean up when we learn things in generalities.

We arrived at the Treblinka rail stop and there was a peaceful calm about the site. Unlike Auschwitz (or other work camps), Treblinka was built for strict extermination. The Nazis built it as part of the Final Solution. The other camps were taking too long to kill, because they were using the people to work, so in order to speed up the process, extermination camps were necessary as well.

Only a handful would survive Treblinka

because immediately upon arrival, they were stripped, shaved, and gassed. George, our guide, told us that the railway leading to the camp looked like any other commercial rail stop in Poland at the time. There was one difference though. The Germans painted a clock on the wall and it always read 6:00 p.m. Time stopped in Treblinka.

We got back in the van to head to the internal camp. Once again, like all the other sites we went to, only symbolic memorials were there to represent what once stood. Treblinka was also in the middle of a vast forest, which made it the perfect site for this kind of operation.

The only true evidence that prove it once stood are aerial pictures. There are a few pictures taken by a German officer of the camp that were put in his memoir called "Beautiful Times." These pictures showed tractors that could have been digging mass graves, but there is no proof of that either. The pictures do not show anything other than the internal

German zoo and some digging pictures

Treblinka was burned to the ground. Now there is just a patch of flattened grassy area in the midst of the trees. The first monuments were tombstone-like and had the names of all the countries the people were brought in from. The central stone was Poland, because the countries people were all brought to this location. A little farther up there were more representative stones. These stones had the names of the towns in Poland where people were from. My father and I put rocks on the town where my grandfather was from. This is a typical gesture in Judaism when you visit the grave site. I think it is supposed to mean that you were there with them.

To be honest, I wasn't an emotional wreck standing there. In other camps, there are barracks still standing and there are tangible pieces to look at and remember. At this camp there was nothing. All you could do was imagine. And you can't imagine. So all you can do is absorb the solemn silence. I had a heavy heart but no tears. It doesn't really hit you until you start to walk away. There is something inside you that doesn't allow you to leave. And then you turn around and see tears in your father's eyes for the first time in your life. When you walk away, it hits you. The silence is the memorial. The nothingness is the memorial.

When you continue walking out through the path, in the trees you can feel the irony.

Where we stood was beautiful. It was as if we were walking through a nature reserve. There has been a recurring theme throughout our trip. We always took notice of the pretty trees surrounding us. The trees have seen so much, and they are the only life that can accurately recall what happened.

We continued our way out. There was something like a "guest book" to sign before leaving the camp. My mom told my dad to write out all the names he could remember and then sign it for the family.

This is when it happened. He started to write and it seemed as if he was going to take up the whole page with lost names. I continued to sit next to him and watch as he wrote name after name of family members that perished in Treblinka. The tears started here. It was then my turn to sign the book. Here is what I wrote:

So many names, none I know...
Danna 8/8/07

ACKNOWLEDGEMENTS

Thank you to my special family. To my beautiful mother who taught me to be outspoken, stand up for myself, and not be afraid to go against the grain. To my father, my genius, who supports my dreams and gracefully passed down my grandparent's stories. To my brother, the other half of this inherited responsibility we have undertaken just by understanding what it means to be a Third Generation.

Thank you to my mentors Dr. Miriam Kassenoff- Klein and Lyanne Wassermann. This work would never have been completed if we didn't meet that fateful day on the first day of class. Your support and knowledge is forever valued.

Thank you to Troy Sorel. Whenever I think it is the end, you show me it's only the beginning. Your love and kindness are my continual life support. Thank you for truly believing in my "voice."

Thank you to all of my family and friends who helped me get to where I am today.

Thank you to all the readers who embrace these messages and take responsibility for disseminating them. We are all in this together.

notes

notes

notes   .